Prayer Journal

for Women

With

The Psalms

Scripture

"He that dwelleth in the secret place of the most High shall abide under the shadow of the Almighty. I will say of the LORD, He is my refuge and my fortress: my God; in him will I trust. Surely he shall deliver thee from the snare of the fowler, and from the noisome pestilence." Psalm 91:1-3

Date _____   Pray For _____

Today's Prayer ✟

_____

_____

_____

_____

_____

_____

_____

Gratitude and Thanks to God for ✟

_____

_____

_____

_____

Take Action (call, write, message) ✟

_____

"Who can find a virtuous woman? for her price is far above rubies." - Proverbs 31:10

Scripture

"He shall cover thee with his feathers, and under his wings shalt thou trust: his truth shall be thy shield and buckler. Thou shalt not be afraid for the terror by night; nor for the arrow that flieth by day; Nor for the pestilence that walketh in darkness; nor for the destruction that wasteth at noonday." - Psalm 91:4-6

Date_____   Pray For_____

Today's Prayer ✞

_____
_____
_____
_____
_____
_____
_____

Gratitude and Thanks to God for ✞

_____
_____
_____
_____
_____

Take Action (call, write, message) ✞

_____

"Who can find a virtuous woman? for her price is far above rubies." - Proverbs 31:10

Scripture

"A thousand shall fall at thy side, and ten thousand at thy right hand; but it shall not come nigh thee. Only with thine eyes shalt thou behold and see the reward of the wicked. Because thou hast made the LORD, which is my refuge, even the most High, thy habitation;" - Psalm 91:7-9

Date_____   Pray For_____

Today's Prayer ✟

_____
_____
_____
_____
_____
_____
_____
_____

Gratitude and Thanks to God for ✟

_____
_____
_____
_____
_____

Take Action (call, write, message) ✟

_____

"Who can find a virtuous woman? for her price is far above rubies." - Proverbs 31:10

Scripture

"There shall no evil befall thee, neither shall any plague come nigh thy dwelling. For he shall give his angels charge over thee, to keep thee in all thy ways. They shall bear thee up in their hands, lest thou dash thy foot against a stone." - Psalm 91:10-12

Date _____   Pray For _____

Today's Prayer ♰

_____
_____
_____
_____
_____
_____
_____

Gratitude and Thanks to God for ♰

_____
_____
_____
_____

Take Action (call, write, message) ♰

_____

"Who can find a virtuous woman? for her price is far above rubies." - Proverbs 31:10

Scripture

"Thou shalt tread upon the lion and adder: the young lion and the dragon shalt thou trample under feet. Because he hath set his love upon me, therefore will I deliver him: I will set him on high, because he hath known my name. He shall call upon me, and I will answer him: I will be with him in trouble; I will deliver him, and honour him." - Psalm 91:13-15

Date_____   Pray For_____

Today's Prayer ✝

_____
_____
_____
_____
_____
_____
_____

Gratitude and Thanks to God for ✝

_____
_____
_____
_____

Take Action (call, write, message) ✝

_____

"Who can find a virtuous woman? for her price is far above rubies." - Proverbs 31:10

Scripture

"Blessed is the man that walketh not in the counsel of the ungodly, nor standeth in the way of sinners, nor sitteth in the seat of the scornful. But his delight is in the law of the LORD; and in his law doth he meditate day and night." - Psalm 1:1-2

Date_____   Pray For_____

Today's Prayer ✝

_____
_____
_____
_____
_____
_____
_____

Gratitude and Thanks to God for ✝

_____
_____
_____
_____

Take Action (call, write, message) ✝

_____

"Who can find a virtuous woman? for her price is far above rubies." - Proverbs 31:10

Scripture

"And he shall be like a tree planted by the rivers of water, that bringeth forth his fruit in his season; his leaf also shall not wither; and whatsoever he doeth shall prosper. ... For the LORD knoweth the way of the righteous: but the way of the ungodly shall perish." - Psalm 1:3, 6

Date _____   Pray For_____

Today's Prayer ☧

_____
_____
_____
_____
_____
_____
_____
_____

Gratitude and Thanks to God for ☧

_____
_____
_____
_____
_____

Take Action (call, write, message) ☧

_____

"Who can find a virtuous woman? for her price is far above rubies." - Proverbs 31:10

Scripture

"But thou, O LORD, art a shield for me; my glory, and the lifter up of mine head. I cried unto the LORD with my voice, and he heard me out of his holy hill. Selah. I laid me down and slept; I awaked; for the LORD sustained me." - Psalm 3:3-5

Date_____   Pray For_____

Today's Prayer ✝

_____
_____
_____
_____
_____
_____
_____

Gratitude and Thanks to God for ✝

_____
_____
_____
_____
_____

Take Action (call, write, message) ✝

_____

"Who can find a virtuous woman? for her price is far above rubies." - Proverbs 31:10

Scripture

"But know that the LORD hath set apart him that is godly for himself: the LORD will hear when I call unto him. Stand in awe, and sin not: commune with your own heart upon your bed, and be still. Selah. Offer the sacrifices of righteousness, and put your trust in the LORD." - Psalm 4:3-5

Date_____ Pray For_____

Today's Prayer ✝

_____
_____
_____
_____
_____
_____
_____
_____

Gratitude and Thanks to God for ✝

_____
_____
_____
_____
_____
_____

Take Action (call, write, message) ✝

_____

"Who can find a virtuous woman? for her price is far above rubies." - Proverbs 31:10

Scripture

"Give ear to my words, O LORD, consider my meditation. Hearken unto the voice of my cry, my King, and my God: for unto thee will I pray. My voice shalt thou hear in the morning, O LORD; in the morning will I direct my prayer unto thee, and will look up. ... For thou, LORD, wilt bless the righteous; with favour wilt thou compass him as with a shield." - Psalm 5:1-3, 12

Date_____   Pray For_____

Today's Prayer ✝

_____
_____
_____
_____
_____
_____
_____

Gratitude and Thanks to God for ✝

_____
_____
_____
_____
_____

Take Action (call, write, message) ✝

_____

"Who can find a virtuous woman? for her price is far above rubies." - Proverbs 31:10

Scripture

"Have mercy upon me, O LORD; for I am weak: O LORD, heal me; for my bones are vexed. ... Return, O LORD, deliver my soul: oh save me for thy mercies' sake. ... The LORD hath heard my supplication; the LORD will receive my prayer." - Psalm 6:2, 4, 9

Date _____   Pray For _____

Today's Prayer ✝

_____
_____
_____
_____
_____
_____
_____

Gratitude and Thanks to God for ✝

_____
_____
_____
_____
_____

Take Action (call, write, message) ✝

_____

"Who can find a virtuous woman? for her price is far above rubies." - Proverbs 31:10

Scripture

"My defence is of God, which saveth the upright in heart. God judgeth the righteous, and God is angry with the wicked every day. ... I will praise the LORD according to his righteousness: and will sing praise to the name of the LORD most high." - Psalm 7:10-11, 17

Date_____   Pray For_____

Today's Prayer ✝

_____
_____
_____
_____
_____
_____
_____
_____

Gratitude and Thanks to God for ✝

_____
_____
_____
_____
_____

Take Action (call, write, message) ✝

_____

"Who can find a virtuous woman? for her price is far above rubies." - Proverbs 31:10

Scripture

"O LORD our Lord, how excellent is thy name in all the earth! who hast set thy glory above the heavens. ... When I consider thy heavens, the work of thy fingers, the moon and the stars, which thou hast ordained; what is man, that thou art mindful of him? and the son of man, that thou visitest him?" - Psalm 8:1, 3-4

Date _____   Pray For _____

Today's Prayer ✝

_____
_____
_____
_____
_____
_____
_____

Gratitude and Thanks to God for ✝

_____
_____
_____
_____

Take Action (call, write, message) ✝

_____

"Who can find a virtuous woman? for her price is far above rubies." - Proverbs 31:10

Scripture

"I will praise thee, O LORD, with my whole heart; I will shew forth all thy marvellous works. I will be glad and rejoice in thee: I will sing praise to thy name, O thou most High. When mine enemies are turned back, they shall fall and perish at thy presence. For thou hast maintained my right and my cause; thou satest in the throne judging right." - Psalm 9:1-4

Date_____   Pray For_____

Today's Prayer ✝

_____
_____
_____
_____
_____
_____
_____
_____

Gratitude and Thanks to God for ✝

_____
_____
_____
_____
_____

Take Action (call, write, message) ✝

_____

"who can find a virtuous woman? for her price is far above rubies." - Proverbs 31:10

Scripture

"Why standest thou afar off, O LORD? why hidest thou thyself in times of trouble? ... Arise, O LORD; O God, lift up thine hand: forget not the humble. ... LORD, thou hast heard the desire of the humble: thou wilt prepare their heart, thou wilt cause thine ear to hear:" - Psalm 10:1, 12, 17

Date _____   Pray For _____

Today's Prayer ✝

_____
_____
_____
_____
_____
_____
_____
_____

Gratitude and Thanks to God for ✝

_____
_____
_____
_____
_____

Take Action (call, write, message) ✝

_____

"Who can find a virtuous woman? for her price is far above rubies." - Proverbs 31:10

Scripture

"In the LORD put I my trust: how say ye to my soul, Flee as a bird to your mountain? ... If the foundations be destroyed, what can the righteous do? ... For the righteous LORD loveth righteousness; his countenance doth behold the upright." - Psalm 11:1, 3, 7

Date_____   Pray For_____

Today's Prayer ☩

_____
_____
_____
_____
_____
_____
_____

Gratitude and Thanks to God for ☩

_____
_____
_____
_____
_____

Take Action (call, write, message) ☩

_____

"Who can find a virtuous woman? for her price is far above rubies." - Proverbs 31:10

Scripture

"The LORD shall cut off all flattering lips, and the tongue that speaketh proud things: ... The words of the LORD are pure words: as silver tried in a furnace of earth, purified seven times. ... The wicked walk on every side, when the vilest men are exalted." - Psalm 12:3, 6, 8

Date _____   Pray For _____

Today's Prayer ✝

_____
_____
_____
_____
_____
_____
_____

Gratitude and Thanks to God for ✝

_____
_____
_____
_____
_____

Take Action (call, write, message) ✝

_____

"Who can find a virtuous woman? for her price is far above rubies." - Proverbs 31:10

Scripture

"Consider and hear me, O LORD my God: lighten mine eyes, lest I sleep the sleep of death; ... But I have trusted in thy mercy; my heart shall rejoice in thy salvation. I will sing unto the LORD, because he hath dealt bountifully with me." - Psalm 13:3, 5-6

Date_____   Pray For_____

Today's Prayer ✞

_____
_____
_____
_____
_____
_____
_____

Gratitude and Thanks to God for ✞

_____
_____
_____
_____
_____

Take Action (call, write, message) ✞

_____

"Who can find a virtuous woman? for her price is far above rubies." - Proverbs 31:10

Scripture

"The fool hath said in his heart, There is no God. They are corrupt, they have done abominable works, there is none that doeth good... Oh that the salvation of Israel were come out of Zion! when the LORD bringeth back the captivity of his people, Jacob shall rejoice, and Israel shall be glad." - Psalm 14:1, 7

Date_____   Pray For_____

Today's Prayer ✝

_____
_____
_____
_____
_____
_____
_____

Gratitude and Thanks to God for ✝

_____
_____
_____
_____
_____

Take Action (call, write, message) ✝

_____

"Who can find a virtuous woman? for her price is far above rubies." - Proverbs 31:10

Scripture

"LORD, who shall abide in thy tabernacle? who shall dwell in thy holy hill? He that walketh uprightly, and worketh righteousness, and speaketh the truth in his heart. ... In whose eyes a vile person is contemned; but he honoureth them that fear the LORD." - Psalm 15:1-2, 4

Date_____   Pray For_____

Today's Prayer ✝

_____
_____
_____
_____
_____
_____
_____
_____

Gratitude and Thanks to God for ✝

_____
_____
_____
_____
_____

Take Action (call, write, message) ✝

_____

"Who can find a virtuous woman? for her price is far above rubies." - Proverbs 31:10

Scripture

"Preserve me, O God: for in thee do I put my trust. O my soul, thou hast said unto the LORD, Thou art my Lord: my goodness extendeth not to thee; But to the saints that are in the earth, and to the excellent, in whom is all my delight." - Psalm 16:1-3

Date_____   Pray For_____

Today's Prayer ✝

_____
_____
_____
_____
_____
_____

Gratitude and Thanks to God for ✝

_____
_____
_____
_____
_____

Take Action (call, write, message) ✝

_____

"Who can find a virtuous woman? for her price is far above rubies." - Proverbs 31:10

Scripture

"The LORD is the portion of mine inheritance and of my cup: thou maintainest my lot. ... I will bless the LORD, who hath given me counsel: my reins also instruct me in the night seasons. I have set the LORD always before me: because he is at my right hand, I shall not be moved." - Psalm 16:5, 7-8

Date_____ Pray For_____

Today's Prayer ✠

_____
_____
_____
_____
_____
_____
_____

Gratitude and Thanks to God for ✠

_____
_____
_____
_____

Take Action (call, write, message) ✠

_____

"Who can find a virtuous woman? for her price is far above rubies." - Proverbs 31:10

Scripture

"Therefore my heart is glad, and my glory rejoiceth: my flesh also shall rest in hope. For thou wilt not leave my soul in hell; neither wilt thou suffer thine Holy One to see corruption. Thou wilt shew me the path of life: in thy presence is fulness of joy; at thy right hand there are pleasures for evermore." - Psalm 16:9-11

Date_____   Pray For_____

Today's Prayer ☩

_____
_____
_____
_____
_____
_____
_____

Gratitude and Thanks to God for ☩

_____
_____
_____
_____
_____

Take Action (call, write, message) ☩

_____

"Who can find a virtuous woman? for her price is far above rubies." - Proverbs 31:10

Scripture

"I have called upon thee, for thou wilt hear me, O God: incline thine ear unto me, and hear my speech. Shew thy marvellous lovingkindness, O thou that savest by thy right hand them which put their trust in thee from those that rise up against them. Keep me as the apple of the eye, hide me under the shadow of thy wings," - Psalm 17:6-8

Date _____   Pray For _____

Today's Prayer ✝

_____

_____

_____

_____

_____

_____

_____

Gratitude and Thanks to God for ✝

_____

_____

_____

_____

_____

Take Action (call, write, message) ✝

_____

"Who can find a virtuous woman? for her price is far above rubies." - Proverbs 31:10

Scripture

"I will love thee, O LORD, my strength. The LORD is my rock, and my fortress, and my deliverer; my God, my strength, in whom I will trust; my buckler, and the horn of my salvation, and my high tower. I will call upon the LORD, who is worthy to be praised: so shall I be saved from mine enemies." - Psalm 18:1-3

Date _____   Pray For _____

Today's Prayer ✝

_____
_____
_____
_____
_____
_____
_____

Gratitude and Thanks to God for ✝

_____
_____
_____
_____
_____

Take Action (call, write, message) ✝

_____

"who can find a virtuous woman? for her price is far above rubies." - Proverbs 31:10

Date_____   Pray For_____

Today's Prayer ✝

_____
_____
_____
_____
_____
_____
_____

Gratitude and Thanks to God for ✝

_____
_____
_____
_____
_____

Take Action (call, write, message) ✝

_____

Scripture

"The LORD hear thee in the day of trouble; the name of the God of Jacob defend thee; ... Grant thee according to thine own heart, and fulfil all thy counsel. We will rejoice in thy salvation, and in the name of our God we will set up our banners: the LORD fulfil all thy petitions." - Psalm 20:1, 4-5

Date _____   Pray For _____

Today's Prayer ✝

_____
_____
_____
_____
_____
_____
_____
_____

Gratitude and Thanks to God for ✝

_____
_____
_____
_____
_____

Take Action (call, write, message) ✝

_____

"Who can find a virtuous woman? for her price is far above rubies." - Proverbs 31:10

Scripture

"The king shall joy in thy strength, O LORD; and in thy salvation how greatly shall he rejoice! Thou hast given him his heart's desire, and hast not withholden the request of his lips. Selah. ... His glory is great in thy salvation: honour and majesty hast thou laid upon him." - Psalm 21:1-2, 5

Date_____   Pray For_____

Today's Prayer ✝

_____
_____
_____
_____
_____
_____
_____

Gratitude and Thanks to God for ✝

_____
_____
_____
_____
_____

Take Action (call, write, message) ✝

_____

"Who can find a virtuous woman? for her price is far above rubies." - Proverbs 31:10

Scripture

"The LORD is my shepherd; I shall not want. He maketh me to lie down in green pastures: he leadeth me beside the still waters. He restoreth my soul: he leadeth me in the paths of righteousness for his name's sake. ... Surely goodness and mercy shall follow me all the days of my life: and I will dwell in the house of the LORD for ever." - Psalm 23:1-3, 6

Date_____   Pray For_____

Today's Prayer ✝

_____
_____
_____
_____
_____
_____
_____
_____

Gratitude and Thanks to God for ✝

_____
_____
_____
_____
_____

Take Action (call, write, message) ✝

_____

"Who can find a virtuous woman? for her price is far above rubies." - Proverbs 31:10

Scripture

"The earth is the LORD'S, and the fulness thereof; the world, and they that dwell therein. ... Who shall ascend into the hill of the LORD? or who shall stand in his holy place? He that hath clean hands, and a pure heart; who hath not lifted up his soul unto vanity, nor sworn deceitfully." - Psalm 24:1, 3-4

Date _____   Pray For _____

Today's Prayer ✝

_____
_____
_____
_____
_____
_____
_____

Gratitude and Thanks to God for ✝

_____
_____
_____
_____
_____

Take Action (call, write, message) ✝

_____

"who can find a virtuous woman? for her price is far above rubies." - Proverbs 31:10

Scripture

"Lift up your heads, O ye gates; and be ye lift up, ye everlasting doors; and the King of glory shall come in. Who is this King of glory? The LORD strong and mighty, the LORD mighty in battle. ... Who is this King of glory? The LORD of hosts, he is the King of glory. Selah." - Psalm 24:7-8, 10

Date_____   Pray For_____

Today's Prayer ✟

_____
_____
_____
_____
_____
_____
_____
_____

Gratitude and Thanks to God for ✟

_____
_____
_____
_____
_____

Take Action (call, write, message) ✟

_____

"Who can find a virtuous woman? for her price is far above rubies." - Proverbs 31:10

Scripture

"Unto thee, O LORD, do I lift up my soul. ... Shew me thy ways, O LORD; teach me thy paths. Lead me in thy truth, and teach me: for thou art the God of my salvation; on thee do I wait all the day. Remember, O LORD, thy tender mercies and thy lovingkindnesses; for they have been ever of old." - Psalm 25:1, 4-6

Date_____   Pray For_____

Today's Prayer ✝

_____
_____
_____
_____
_____
_____
_____

Gratitude and Thanks to God for ✝

_____
_____
_____
_____

Take Action (call, write, message) ✝

_____

"Who can find a virtuous woman? for her price is far above rubies." - Proverbs 31:10

Scripture

"All the paths of the LORD are mercy and truth unto such as keep his covenant and his testimonies. For thy name's sake, O LORD, pardon mine iniquity; for it is great. ... The secret of the LORD is with them that fear him; and he will shew them his covenant." - Psalm 25:10-11, 14

Date_____   Pray For_____

Today's Prayer ✝

_____
_____
_____
_____
_____
_____
_____

Gratitude and Thanks to God for ✝

_____
_____
_____
_____
_____

Take Action (call, write, message) ✝

_____

"Who can find a virtuous woman? for her price is far above rubies." - Proverbs 31:10

Scripture

"Judge me, O LORD; for I have walked in mine integrity: I have trusted also in the LORD; therefore I shall not slide. Examine me, O LORD, and prove me; try my reins and my heart. For thy lovingkindness is before mine eyes: and I have walked in thy truth." - Psalm 26:1-3

Date _____ Pray For _____

Today's Prayer ✝

_____
_____
_____
_____
_____
_____
_____

Gratitude and Thanks to God for ✝

_____
_____
_____
_____
_____

Take Action (call, write, message) ✝

_____

"Who can find a virtuous woman? for her price is far above rubies." - Proverbs 31:10

Scripture

"The LORD is my light and my salvation; whom shall I fear? the LORD is the strength of my life; of whom shall I be afraid? ... Hear, O LORD, when I cry with my voice: have mercy also upon me, and answer me. When thou saidst, Seek ye my face; my heart said unto thee, Thy face, LORD, will I seek." - Psalm 27:1, 7-8

Date _____   Pray For _____

Today's Prayer ✝

_____
_____
_____
_____
_____
_____
_____

Gratitude and Thanks to God for ✝

_____
_____
_____
_____
_____

Take Action (call, write, message) ✝

_____

"Who can find a virtuous woman? for her price is far above rubies." - Proverbs 31:10

Scripture

"Blessed be the LORD, because he hath heard the voice of my supplications. The LORD is my strength and my shield; my heart trusted in him, and I am helped: therefore my heart greatly rejoiceth; and with my song will I praise him. The LORD is their strength, and he is the saving strength of his anointed." - Psalm 28:6-8

Date_____   Pray For_____

Today's Prayer ✝

_____
_____
_____
_____
_____
_____
_____
_____

Gratitude and Thanks to God for ✝

_____
_____
_____
_____
_____

Take Action (call, write, message) ✝

_____

"Who can find a virtuous woman? for her price is far above rubies." - Proverbs 31:10

Scripture

"Give unto the LORD, O ye mighty, give unto the LORD glory and strength. Give unto the LORD the glory due unto his name; worship the LORD in the beauty of holiness. ... The voice of the LORD is powerful; the voice of the LORD is full of majesty." - Psalm 29:1-2, 4

Date_____   Pray For_____

Today's Prayer ✝

_____
_____
_____
_____
_____
_____
_____

Gratitude and Thanks to God for ✝

_____
_____
_____
_____
_____

Take Action (call, write, message) ✝

_____

"Who can find a virtuous woman? for her price is far above rubies." - Proverbs 31:10

Scripture

"O LORD my God, I cried unto thee, and thou hast healed me. ... Sing unto the LORD, O ye saints of his, and give thanks at the remembrance of his holiness. ... I cried to thee, O LORD; and unto the LORD I made supplication. ... Hear, O LORD, and have mercy upon me: LORD, be thou my helper."
- Psalm 30:2, 4, 8, 10

Date_____   Pray For_____

Today's Prayer ✝

_____
_____
_____
_____
_____
_____
_____

Gratitude and Thanks to God for ✝

_____
_____
_____
_____
_____

Take Action (call, write, message) ✝

_____

"Who can find a virtuous woman? for her price is far above rubies." - Proverbs 31:10

Scripture

"In thee, O LORD, do I put my trust; let me never be ashamed: deliver me in thy righteousness. Bow down thine ear to me; deliver me speedily: be thou my strong rock, for an house of defence to save me. For thou art my rock and my fortress; therefore for thy name's sake lead me, and guide me." - Psalm 31:1-3

Date_____   Pray For_____

Today's Prayer ♰

_____
_____
_____
_____
_____
_____
_____
_____

Gratitude and Thanks to God for ♰

_____
_____
_____
_____
_____

Take Action (call, write, message) ♰

_____

"Who can find a virtuous woman? for her price is far above rubies." - Proverbs 31:10

Scripture

"Blessed is he whose transgression is forgiven, whose sin is covered. Blessed is the man unto whom the LORD imputeth not iniquity, and in whose spirit there is no guile. ... Be glad in the LORD, and rejoice, ye righteous: and shout for joy, all ye that are upright in heart." - Psalm 32:1-2, 11

Date_____   Pray For_____

Today's Prayer ✝

_____
_____
_____
_____
_____
_____
_____

Gratitude and Thanks to God for ✝

_____
_____
_____
_____
_____

Take Action (call, write, message) ✝

_____

"Who can find a virtuous woman? for her price is far above rubies." - Proverbs 31:10

Scripture

"Behold, the eye of the LORD is upon them that fear him, upon them that hope in his mercy; To deliver their soul from death, and to keep them alive in famine. Our soul waiteth for the LORD: he is our help and our shield. For our heart shall rejoice in him, because we have trusted in his holy name." - Psalm 33:18-21

Date_____   Pray For_____

Today's Prayer ✝

_____
_____
_____
_____
_____
_____
_____

Gratitude and Thanks to God for ✝

_____
_____
_____
_____
_____

Take Action (call, write, message) ✝

_____

"Who can find a virtuous woman? for her price is far above rubies." - Proverbs 31:10

Scripture

"I will bless the LORD at all times: his praise shall continually be in my mouth. ... O magnify the LORD with me, and let us exalt his name together. I sought the LORD, and he heard me, and delivered me from all my fears. ... The LORD is nigh unto them that are of a broken heart; and saveth such as be of a contrite spirit." - Psalm 34:1, 3-4, 18

Date_____   Pray For_____

Today's Prayer ✝

_____
_____
_____
_____
_____
_____
_____

Gratitude and Thanks to God for ✝

_____
_____
_____
_____
_____

Take Action (call, write, message) ✝

_____

"Who can find a virtuous woman? for her price is far above rubies." - Proverbs 31:10

Scripture

"Thy mercy, O LORD, is in the heavens; and thy faithfulness reacheth unto the clouds... How excellent is thy lovingkindness, O God! therefore the children of men put their trust under the shadow of thy wings. ... For with thee is the fountain of life: in thy light shall we see light." - Psalm 36:5, 7, 9

Date_____   Pray For_____

Today's Prayer ☩

_____
_____
_____
_____
_____
_____
_____

Gratitude and Thanks to God for ☩

_____
_____
_____
_____
_____

Take Action (call, write, message) ☩

_____

"Who can find a virtuous woman? for her price is far above rubies." - Proverbs 31:10

Scripture

"Delight thyself also in the LORD; and he shall give thee the desires of thine heart. Commit thy way unto the LORD; trust also in him; and he shall bring it to pass... The steps of a good man are ordered by the LORD: and he delighteth in his way... But the salvation of the righteous is of the LORD: he is their strength in the time of trouble." - Psalm 37:4-5, 23, 39

Date_____   Pray For_____

Today's Prayer ✟

_____
_____
_____
_____
_____
_____

Gratitude and Thanks to God for ✟

_____
_____
_____
_____

Take Action (call, write, message) ✟

_____

"Who can find a virtuous woman? for her price is far above rubies." - Proverbs 31:10

Scripture

"For in thee, O LORD, do I hope: thou wilt hear, O Lord my God. ... For I will declare mine iniquity; I will be sorry for my sin. ... Forsake me not, O LORD: O my God, be not far from me. Make haste to help me, O Lord my salvation." - Psalm 38:15, 18, 21-22

Date _____   Pray For _____

Today's Prayer ✝

_____
_____
_____
_____
_____
_____
_____

Gratitude and Thanks to God for ✝

_____
_____
_____
_____
_____

Take Action (call, write, message) ✝

_____

"Who can find a virtuous woman? for her price is far above rubies." - Proverbs 31:10

Scripture

"Sacrifice and offering thou didst not desire; mine ears hast thou opened: burnt offering and sin offering hast thou not required. Then said I, Lo, I come: in the volume of the book it is written of me, I delight to do thy will, O my God: yea, thy law is within my heart." - Psalm 40:6-8 KJV

Date_____   Pray For_____

Today's Prayer ✟

_____
_____
_____
_____
_____
_____
_____

Gratitude and Thanks to God for ✟

_____
_____
_____
_____
_____

Take Action (call, write, message) ✟

_____

"Who can find a virtuous woman? for her price is far above rubies." - Proverbs 31:10

Scripture

"As the hart panteth after the water brooks, so panteth my soul after thee, O God. My soul thirsteth for God, for the living God: when shall I come and appear before God? ... Yet the LORD will command his lovingkindness in the daytime, and in the night his song shall be with me, and my prayer unto the God of my life." - Psalm 42:1-2, 8

Date_____   Pray For_____

Today's Prayer ✝

_____
_____
_____
_____
_____
_____
_____

Gratitude and Thanks to God for ✝

_____
_____
_____
_____
_____

Take Action (call, write, message) ✝

_____

"Who can find a virtuous woman? for her price is far above rubies." - Proverbs 31:10

Scripture

"Thy throne, O God, is for ever and ever: the sceptre of thy kingdom is a right sceptre. Thou lovest righteousness, and hatest wickedness: therefore God, thy God, hath anointed thee with the oil of gladness above thy fellows. All thy garments smell of myrrh, and aloes, and cassia, out of the ivory palaces, whereby they have made thee glad." - Psalm 45:6-8

Date _____   Pray For _____

Today's Prayer ✝

_____
_____
_____
_____
_____
_____
_____

Gratitude and Thanks to God for ✝

_____
_____
_____
_____

Take Action (call, write, message) ✝

_____

"Who can find a virtuous woman? for her price is far above rubies." - Proverbs 31:10

Scripture

"God is our refuge and strength, a very present help in trouble. Therefore will not we fear, though the earth be removed, and though the mountains be carried into the midst of the sea; ... Be still, and know that I am God: I will be exalted among the heathen, I will be exalted in the earth." - Psalm 46:1-2, 10

Date_____   Pray For_____

Today's Prayer ✝

_____
_____
_____
_____
_____
_____
_____

Gratitude and Thanks to God for ✝

_____
_____
_____
_____
_____

Take Action (call, write, message) ✝

_____

"Who can find a virtuous woman? for her price is far above rubies." - Proverbs 31:10

Scripture

"God is gone up with a shout, the LORD with the sound of a trumpet. Sing praises to God, sing praises: sing praises unto our King, sing praises. For God is the King of all the earth: sing ye praises with understanding. God reigneth over the heathen: God sitteth upon the throne of his holiness." - Psalm 47:5-8

Date_____   Pray For_____

Today's Prayer ☩

_____
_____
_____
_____
_____
_____
_____

Gratitude and Thanks to God for ☩

_____
_____
_____
_____
_____

Take Action (call, write, message) ☩

_____

"Who can find a virtuous woman? for her price is far above rubies." - Proverbs 31:10

Scripture

"Great is the LORD, and greatly to be praised in the city of our God, in the mountain of his holiness. Beautiful for situation, the joy of the whole earth, is mount Zion, on the sides of the north, the city of the great King. ... According to thy name, O God, so is thy praise unto the ends of the earth: thy right hand is full of righteousness." - Psalm 48:1-2, 10 KJV

Date _____   Pray For _____

Today's Prayer ♰

_____
_____
_____
_____
_____
_____
_____

Gratitude and Thanks to God for ♰

_____
_____
_____
_____
_____

Take Action (call, write, message) ♰

_____

"Who can find a virtuous woman? for her price is far above rubies." - Proverbs 31:10

Scripture

"Have mercy upon me, O God, according to thy lovingkindness: according unto the multitude of thy tender mercies blot out my transgressions... Create in me a clean heart, O God; and renew a right spirit within me... The sacrifices of God are a broken spirit: a broken and a contrite heart, O God, thou wilt not despise." - Psalm 51:1, 10, 17

Date_____   Pray For_____

Today's Prayer ✝

_____
_____
_____
_____
_____
_____
_____

Gratitude and Thanks to God for ✝

_____
_____
_____
_____

Take Action (call, write, message) ✝

_____

"Who can find a virtuous woman? for her price is far above rubies." - Proverbs 31:10

Scripture

"Save me, O God, by thy name, and judge me by thy strength. Hear my prayer, O God; give ear to the words of my mouth... Behold, God is mine helper: the Lord is with them that uphold my soul... For he hath delivered me out of all trouble: and mine eye hath seen his desire upon mine enemies." - Psalm 54:1-2, 4, 7

Date_____   Pray For_____

Today's Prayer ✝

_____
_____
_____
_____
_____
_____
_____

Gratitude and Thanks to God for ✝

_____
_____
_____
_____
_____

Take Action (call, write, message) ✝

_____

"Who can find a virtuous woman? for her price is far above rubies." - Proverbs 31:10

Scripture

"Give ear to my prayer, O God; and hide not thyself from my supplication. ... And I said, Oh that I had wings like a dove! for then would I fly away, and be at rest. ... As for me, I will call upon God; and the LORD shall save me. ... Cast thy burden upon the LORD, and he shall sustain thee: he shall never suffer the righteous to be moved." - Psalm 55:1, 6, 16, 22

Date_____   Pray For_____

Today's Prayer ✝

_____
_____
_____
_____
_____
_____
_____

Gratitude and Thanks to God for ✝

_____
_____
_____
_____
_____

Take Action (call, write, message) ✝

_____

"Who can find a virtuous woman? for her price is far above rubies." - Proverbs 31:10

Scripture

"In God will I praise his word: in the LORD will I praise his word. In God have I put my trust: I will not be afraid what man can do unto me. Thy vows are upon me, O God: I will render praises unto thee. For thou hast delivered my soul from death: wilt not thou deliver my feet from falling, that I may walk before God in the light of the living?" - Psalm 56:10-13

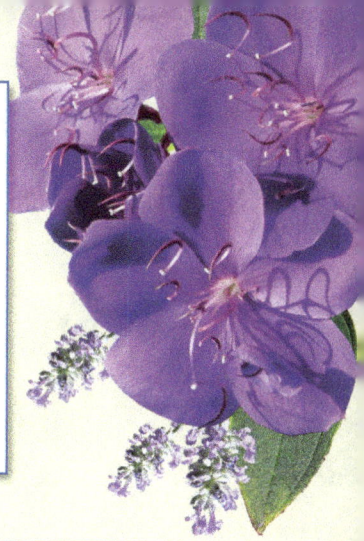

Date_____   Pray For_____

Today's Prayer ✝

_____

_____

_____

_____

_____

_____

_____

Gratitude and Thanks to God for ✝

_____

_____

_____

_____

Take Action (call, write, message) ✝

_____

"Who can find a virtuous woman? for her price is far above rubies." - Proverbs 31:10

Scripture

"Be thou exalted, O God, above the heavens; let thy glory be above all the earth. ... My heart is fixed, O God, my heart is fixed: I will sing and give praise. ... I will praise thee, O Lord, among the people: I will sing unto thee among the nations. ... Be thou exalted, O God, above the heavens: let thy glory be above all the earth." - Psalm 57:5, 7, 9, 11

Date_____   Pray For_____

Today's Prayer ✝

_____
_____
_____
_____
_____
_____
_____

Gratitude and Thanks to God for ✝

_____
_____
_____
_____
_____

Take Action (call, write, message) ✝

_____

"Who can find a virtuous woman? for her price is far above rubies." - Proverbs 31:10

Scripture

"Hear my cry, O God; attend unto my prayer. ... For thou hast been a shelter for me, and a strong tower from the enemy. I will abide in thy tabernacle for ever: I will trust in the covert of thy wings. Selah. ... He shall abide before God for ever: O prepare mercy and truth, which may preserve him." - Psalm 61:1, 3-4, 7

Date_____   Pray For_____

Today's Prayer ✝

_____
_____
_____
_____
_____
_____
_____

Gratitude and Thanks to God for ✝

_____
_____
_____
_____
_____

Take Action (call, write, message) ✝

_____

"Who can find a virtuous woman? for her price is far above rubies." - Proverbs 31:10

Scripture

"Truly my soul waiteth upon God: from him cometh my salvation. He only is my rock and my salvation; he is my defence; I shall not be greatly moved. ... Trust in him at all times; ye people, pour out your heart before him: God is a refuge for us. Selah. ... God hath spoken once; twice have I heard this; that power belongeth unto God." - Psalm 62:1-2, 8, 11

Date_____   Pray For_____

Today's Prayer ✝
_____
_____
_____
_____
_____
_____
_____

Gratitude and Thanks to God for ✝
_____
_____
_____
_____

Take Action (call, write, message) ✝
_____

"Who can find a virtuous woman? for her price is far above rubies." - Proverbs 31:10

Scripture

"O God, thou art my God; early will I seek thee: my soul thirsteth for thee, my flesh longeth for thee in a dry and thirsty land, where no water is; To see thy power and thy glory, so as I have seen thee in the sanctuary. Because thy lovingkindness is better than life, my lips shall praise thee." - Psalm 63:1-3

Date _____   Pray For _____

Today's Prayer ✠

_____
_____
_____
_____
_____
_____
_____
_____

Gratitude and Thanks to God for ✠

_____
_____
_____
_____
_____

Take Action (call, write, message) ✠

_____

"Who can find a virtuous woman? for her price is far above rubies." - Proverbs 31:10

Scripture

"Thus will I bless thee while I live: I will lift up my hands in thy name. My soul shall be satisfied as with marrow and fatness; and my mouth shall praise thee with joyful lips: When I remember thee upon my bed, and meditate on thee in the night watches. Because thou hast been my help, therefore in the shadow of thy wings will I rejoice." - Psalm 63:4-7

Date_____   Pray For_____

Today's Prayer ☩

_____
_____
_____
_____
_____
_____
_____
_____

Gratitude and Thanks to God for ☩

_____
_____
_____
_____
_____

Take Action (call, write, message) ☩

_____

"Who can find a virtuous woman? for her price is far above rubies." - Proverbs 31:10

Scripture

"Hear my voice, O God, in my prayer: preserve my life from fear of the enemy. ... And all men shall fear, and shall declare the work of God; for they shall wisely consider of his doing. The righteous shall be glad in the LORD, and shall trust in him; and all the upright in heart shall glory." - Psalm 64:1, 9-10

Date _____   Pray For _____

Today's Prayer ✝

_____
_____
_____
_____
_____
_____
_____

Gratitude and Thanks to God for ✝

_____
_____
_____
_____
_____

Take Action (call, write, message) ✝

_____

"Who can find a virtuous woman? for her price is far above rubies." - Proverbs 31:10

Scripture

"Make a joyful noise unto God, all ye lands: Sing forth the honour of his name: make his praise glorious. ... All the earth shall worship thee, and shall sing unto thee; they shall sing to thy name. Selah. ... O bless our God, ye people, and make the voice of his praise to be heard." - Psalm 66:1-2, 4, 8

Date_____   Pray For_____

Today's Prayer ✝

_____
_____
_____
_____
_____
_____
_____

Gratitude and Thanks to God for ✝

_____
_____
_____
_____
_____

Take Action (call, write, message) ✝

_____

"Who can find a virtuous woman? for her price is far above rubies." - Proverbs 31:10

Scripture

"For thou, O God, hast proved us: thou hast tried us, as silver is tried. ... Come and hear, all ye that fear God, and I will declare what he hath done for my soul. ... If I regard iniquity in my heart, the Lord will not hear me: ... Blessed be God, which hath not turned away my prayer, nor his mercy from me." - Psalm 66:10, 16, 18, 20

Date_____   Pray For_____

Today's Prayer ✝

_____
_____
_____
_____
_____
_____
_____

Gratitude and Thanks to God for ✝

_____
_____
_____
_____
_____

Take Action (call, write, message) ✝

_____

"Who can find a virtuous woman? for her price is far above rubies." - Proverbs 31:10

Scripture

"God be merciful unto us, and bless us; and cause his face to shine upon us; Selah. That thy way may be known upon earth, thy saving health among all nations. Let the people praise thee, O God; let all the people praise thee." - Psalm 67:1-3

Date_____   Pray For_____

Today's Prayer ✝

_____
_____
_____
_____
_____
_____
_____

Gratitude and Thanks to God for ✝

_____
_____
_____
_____
_____

Take Action (call, write, message) ✝

_____

"Who can find a virtuous woman? for her price is far above rubies." - Proverbs 31:10

Scripture

"Blessed be the Lord, who daily loadeth us with benefits, even the God of our salvation. Selah... Sing unto God, ye kingdoms of the earth; O sing praises unto the Lord; Selah: To him that rideth upon the heavens of heavens, which were of old; lo, he doth send out his voice, and that a mighty voice." - Psalm 68:19, 32-33

Date_____   Pray For_____

Today's Prayer ✝

_____
_____
_____
_____
_____
_____
_____

Gratitude and Thanks to God for ✝

_____
_____
_____
_____
_____

Take Action (call, write, message) ✝

_____

"Who can find a virtuous woman? for her price is far above rubies." - Proverbs 31:10

Scripture

"But as for me, my prayer is unto thee, O LORD, in an acceptable time: O God, in the multitude of thy mercy hear me, in the truth of thy salvation... Hear me, O LORD; for thy lovingkindness is good: turn unto me according to the multitude of thy tender mercies... I will praise the name of God with a song, and will magnify him with thanksgiving." - Psalm 69:13, 16, 30

Date_____   Pray For_____

Today's Prayer ✞

_____
_____
_____
_____
_____
_____
_____
_____

Gratitude and Thanks to God for ✞

_____
_____
_____
_____

Take Action (call, write, message) ✞

_____

"who can find a virtuous woman? for her price is far above rubies." - Proverbs 31:10

Scripture

"In thee, O LORD, do I put my trust: let me never be put to confusion. Deliver me in thy righteousness, and cause me to escape: incline thine ear unto me, and save me. Be thou my strong habitation, whereunto I may continually resort: thou hast given commandment to save me; for thou art my rock and my fortress." - Psalm 71:1-3

Date _____   Pray For _____

Today's Prayer ✟

_____
_____
_____
_____
_____
_____
_____

Gratitude and Thanks to God for ✟

_____
_____
_____
_____
_____

Take Action (call, write, message) ✟

_____

"Who can find a virtuous woman? for her price is far above rubies." - Proverbs 31:10

"Deliver me, O my God, out of the hand of the wicked, out of the hand of the unrighteous and cruel man. For thou art my hope, O Lord GOD: thou art my trust from my youth. ... Let my mouth be filled with thy praise and with thy honour all the day." - Psalm 71:4-5, 8

Date_____   Pray For_____

Today's Prayer ✝

_____
_____
_____
_____
_____
_____
_____

Gratitude and Thanks to God for ✝

_____
_____
_____
_____
_____

Take Action (call, write, message) ✝

_____

"Who can find a virtuous woman? for her price is far above rubies." - Proverbs 31:10

Scripture

"O God, be not far from me: O my God, make haste for my help. ... But I will hope continually, and will yet praise thee more and more. ... I will go in the strength of the Lord GOD: I will make mention of thy righteousness, even of thine only. ... My lips shall greatly rejoice when I sing unto thee; and my soul, which thou hast redeemed." - Psalm 71:12, 14, 16, 23

Date_____   Pray For_____

Today's Prayer ♰

_____
_____
_____
_____
_____
_____
_____
_____

Gratitude and Thanks to God for ♰

_____
_____
_____
_____
_____

Take Action (call, write, message) ♰

_____

"Who can find a virtuous woman? for her price is far above rubies." - Proverbs 31:10

Scripture

"Nevertheless I am continually with thee: thou hast holden me by my right hand. Thou shalt guide me with thy counsel, and afterward receive me to glory. Whom have I in heaven but thee? and there is none upon earth that I desire beside thee. ... But it is good for me to draw near to God: I have put my trust in the Lord GOD, that I may declare all thy works." - Psalm 73:23-25, 28

Date_____   Pray For_____

Today's Prayer ✝

_____
_____
_____
_____
_____
_____
_____

Gratitude and Thanks to God for ✝

_____
_____
_____
_____
_____

Take Action (call, write, message) ✝

_____

"Who can find a virtuous woman? for her price is far above rubies." - Proverbs 31:10

Scripture

"I cried unto God with my voice, even unto God with my voice; and he gave ear unto me. In the day of my trouble I sought the Lord: my sore ran in the night, and ceased not: my soul refused to be comforted. I remembered God, and was troubled: I complained, and my spirit was overwhelmed. Selah." - Psalm 77:1-3

Date _____   Pray For _____

Today's Prayer ✠

_____
_____
_____
_____
_____
_____
_____

Gratitude and Thanks to God for ✠

_____
_____
_____
_____
_____

Take Action (call, write, message) ✠

_____

"Who can find a virtuous woman? for her price is far above rubies." - Proverbs 31:10

Scripture

"I will remember the works of the LORD: surely I will remember thy wonders of old. I will meditate also of all thy work, and talk of thy doings. Thy way, O God, is in the sanctuary: who is so great a God as our God? Thou art the God that doest wonders: thou hast declared thy strength among the people." - Psalm 77:11-14

Date_____   Pray For_____

Today's Prayer ✝

_____
_____
_____
_____
_____
_____
_____
_____
_____

Gratitude and Thanks to God for ✝

_____
_____
_____
_____
_____

Take Action (call, write, message) ✝

_____

"who can find a virtuous woman? for her price is far above rubies." - Proverbs 31:10

Scripture

"Sing aloud unto God our strength: make a joyful noise unto the God of Jacob. ... Blow up the trumpet in the new moon, in the time appointed, on our solemn feast day. ... I am the LORD thy God, which brought thee out of the land of Egypt: open thy mouth wide, and I will fill it." - Psalm 81:1, 3, 10

Date_____   Pray For_____

Today's Prayer ✝

_____
_____
_____
_____
_____
_____
_____

Gratitude and Thanks to God for ✝

_____
_____
_____
_____
_____

Take Action (call, write, message) ✝

_____

"Who can find a virtuous woman? for her price is far above rubies." - Proverbs 31:10

Scripture

"Blessed are they that dwell in thy house: they will be still praising thee. Selah. Blessed is the man whose strength is in thee; in whose heart are the ways of them. ... Behold, O God our shield, and look upon the face of thine anointed. ... O LORD of hosts, blessed is the man that trusteth in thee." - Psalm 84:4-5, 9, 12

Date_____   Pray For_____

Today's Prayer ✝

_____
_____
_____
_____
_____
_____
_____

Gratitude and Thanks to God for ✝

_____
_____
_____
_____
_____

Take Action (call, write, message) ✝

_____

"Who can find a virtuous woman? for her price is far above rubies." - Proverbs 31:10

Scripture

"Shew us thy mercy, O LORD, and grant us thy salvation. I will hear what God the LORD will speak: for he will speak peace unto his people, and to his saints: but let them not turn again to folly. Surely his salvation is nigh them that fear him; that glory may dwell in our land." - Psalm 85:7-9

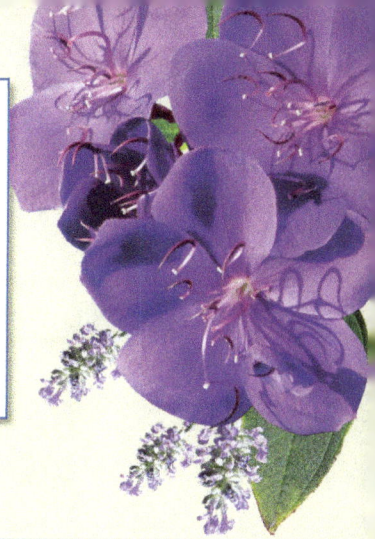

Date _____   Pray For _____

Today's Prayer ✝

_____
_____
_____
_____
_____
_____
_____

Gratitude and Thanks to God for ✝

_____
_____
_____
_____
_____

Take Action (call, write, message) ✝

_____

"Who can find a virtuous woman? for her price is far above rubies." - Proverbs 31:10

Scripture

"Mercy and truth are met together; righteousness and peace have kissed each other. ... Yea, the LORD shall give that which is good; and our land shall yield her increase. Righteousness shall go before him; and shall set us in the way of his steps." - Psalm 85:10, 12-13

Date_____   Pray For_____

Today's Prayer ✝

_____
_____
_____
_____
_____
_____
_____
_____

Gratitude and Thanks to God for ✝

_____
_____
_____
_____
_____

Take Action (call, write, message) ✝

_____

"Who can find a virtuous woman? for her price is far above rubies." - Proverbs 31:10

Scripture

"Bow down thine ear, O LORD, hear me: for I am poor and needy. Preserve my soul; for I am holy: O thou my God, save thy servant that trusteth in thee. Be merciful unto me, O Lord: for I cry unto thee daily. Rejoice the soul of thy servant: for unto thee, O Lord, do I lift up my soul." - Psalm 86:1-4

Date_____   Pray For_____

Today's Prayer ✟

_____
_____
_____
_____
_____
_____
_____

Gratitude and Thanks to God for ✟

_____
_____
_____
_____
_____

Take Action (call, write, message) ✟

_____

"Who can find a virtuous woman? for her price is far above rubies." - Proverbs 31:10

Scripture

"For thou, Lord, art good, and ready to forgive; and plenteous in mercy unto all them that call upon thee. Give ear, O LORD, unto my prayer; and attend to the voice of my supplications. In the day of my trouble I will call upon thee: for thou wilt answer me." - Psalm 86:5-7 KJV

Date_____   Pray For_____

Today's Prayer ✝

_____
_____
_____
_____
_____
_____
_____

Gratitude and Thanks to God for ✝

_____
_____
_____
_____
_____

Take Action (call, write, message) ✝

_____

"Who can find a virtuous woman? for her price is far above rubies." - Proverbs 31:10

Scripture

"Among the gods there is none like unto thee, O Lord; neither are there any works like unto thy works. All nations whom thou hast made shall come and worship before thee, O Lord; and shall glorify thy name. For thou art great, and doest wondrous things: thou art God alone." - Psalm 86:8-10

Date _____ Pray For _____

Today's Prayer ✝

_____
_____
_____
_____
_____
_____
_____

Gratitude and Thanks to God for ✝

_____
_____
_____
_____
_____

Take Action (call, write, message) ✝

_____

"Who can find a virtuous woman? for her price is far above rubies." - Proverbs 31:10

Scripture

"Teach me thy way, O LORD; I will walk in thy truth: unite my heart to fear thy name. I will praise thee, O Lord my God, with all my heart: and I will glorify thy name for evermore. For great is thy mercy toward me: and thou hast delivered my soul from the lowest hell." - Psalm 86:11-13

Date_____   Pray For_____

Today's Prayer ✝

_____
_____
_____
_____
_____
_____
_____

Gratitude and Thanks to God for ✝

_____
_____
_____
_____
_____

Take Action (call, write, message) ✝

_____

"Who can find a virtuous woman? for her price is far above rubies." - Proverbs 31:10

Scripture

"But thou, O Lord, art a God full of compassion, and gracious, longsuffering, and plenteous in mercy and truth. O turn unto me, and have mercy upon me; give thy strength unto thy servant, and save the son of thine handmaid." - Psalm 86:15–16

Date _____   Pray For _____

Today's Prayer ✝

_____

_____

_____

_____

_____

_____

_____

Gratitude and Thanks to God for ✝

_____

_____

_____

_____

_____

Take Action (call, write, message) ✝

_____

"Who can find a virtuous woman? for her price is far above rubies." - Proverbs 31:10

Scripture

"O LORD God of my salvation, I have cried day and night before thee: Let my prayer come before thee: incline thine ear unto my cry; ... But unto thee have I cried, O LORD; and in the morning shall my prayer come before thee." - Psalm 88:1-2, 13 KJV

Date _____   Pray For _____

Today's Prayer ✝

_____
_____
_____
_____
_____
_____
_____

Gratitude and Thanks to God for ✝

_____
_____
_____
_____

Take Action (call, write, message) ✝

_____

"Who can find a virtuous woman? for her price is far above rubies." - Proverbs 31:10

Scripture

"I will sing of the mercies of the LORD for ever: with my mouth will I make known thy faithfulness to all generations. For I have said, Mercy shall be built up for ever: thy faithfulness shalt thou establish in the very heavens... And the heavens shall praise thy wonders, O LORD: thy faithfulness also in the congregation of the saints." - Psalm 89:1-2, 5

Date _____   Pray For _____

Today's Prayer ✝

_____
_____
_____
_____
_____
_____
_____

Gratitude and Thanks to God for ✝

_____
_____
_____
_____
_____

Take Action (call, write, message) ✝

_____

"Who can find a virtuous woman? for her price is far above rubies." - Proverbs 31:10

Scripture

"O LORD God of hosts, who is a strong LORD like unto thee? or to thy faithfulness round about thee? ... The heavens are thine, the earth also is thine: as for the world and the fulness thereof, thou hast founded them. ... Justice and judgment are the habitation of thy throne: mercy and truth shall go before thy face." - Psalm 89:8, 11, 14

Date_____   Pray For_____

Today's Prayer ✝
_____
_____
_____
_____
_____
_____
_____
_____

Gratitude and Thanks to God for ✝
_____
_____
_____
_____
_____

Take Action (call, write, message) ✝
_____

"Who can find a virtuous woman? for her price is far above rubies." - Proverbs 31:10

Scripture

"Blessed is the people that know the joyful sound: they shall walk, O LORD, in the light of thy countenance. In thy name shall they rejoice all the day: and in thy righteousness shall they be exalted. For thou art the glory of their strength: and in thy favour our horn shall be exalted." - Psalm 89:15–17

Date_____   Pray For_____

Today's Prayer ♰

_____
_____
_____
_____
_____
_____
_____

Gratitude and Thanks to God for ♰

_____
_____
_____
_____
_____

Take Action (call, write, message) ♰

_____

"Who can find a virtuous woman? for her price is far above rubies." - Proverbs 31:10

Scripture

"Lord, thou hast been our dwelling place in all generations. ... O satisfy us early with thy mercy; that we may rejoice and be glad all our days. ... And let the beauty of the LORD our God be upon us: and establish thou the work of our hands upon us; yea, the work of our hands establish thou it." - Psalm 90:1, 14, 17

Date _____   Pray For _____

Today's Prayer ✝

_____
_____
_____
_____
_____
_____
_____

Gratitude and Thanks to God for ✝

_____
_____
_____
_____
_____

Take Action (call, write, message) ✝

_____

"Who can find a virtuous woman? for her price is far above rubies." - Proverbs 31:10

Scripture

"It is a good thing to give thanks unto the LORD, and to sing praises unto thy name, O most High: To shew forth thy lovingkindness in the morning, and thy faithfulness every night, ... For thou, LORD, hast made me glad through thy work: I will triumph in the works of thy hands." - Psalm 92:1-2, 4

Date_____ Pray For_____

Today's Prayer ✝

_____
_____
_____
_____
_____
_____
_____
_____

Gratitude and Thanks to God for ✝

_____
_____
_____
_____
_____

Take Action (call, write, message) ✝

_____

"Who can find a virtuous woman? for her price is far above rubies." - Proverbs 31:10

Scripture

"The righteous shall flourish like the palm tree: he shall grow like a cedar in Lebanon. Those that be planted in the house of the LORD shall flourish in the courts of our God. ... To shew that the LORD is upright: he is my rock, and there is no unrighteousness in him." - Psalm 92:12-13, 15

Date_____   Pray For_____

Today's Prayer ✝

_____
_____
_____
_____
_____
_____
_____

Gratitude and Thanks to God for ✝

_____
_____
_____
_____

Take Action (call, write, message) ✝

_____

"Who can find a virtuous woman? for her price is far above rubies." - Proverbs 31:10

Scripture

"The LORD reigneth, he is clothed with majesty; the LORD is clothed with strength, wherewith he hath girded himself: the world also is stablished, that it cannot be moved... The LORD on high is mightier than the noise of many waters, yea, than the mighty waves of the sea. Thy testimonies are very sure: holiness becometh thine house, O LORD, for ever." - Psalm 93:1, 4-5

Date_____   Pray For_____

Today's Prayer ✝

_____
_____
_____
_____
_____
_____
_____

Gratitude and Thanks to God for ✝

_____
_____
_____
_____
_____

Take Action (call, write, message) ✝

_____

"Who can find a virtuous woman? for her price is far above rubies." - Proverbs 31:10

"O come, let us sing unto the LORD: let us make a joyful noise to the rock of our salvation. Let us come before his presence with thanksgiving, and make a joyful noise unto him with psalms. For the LORD is a great God, and a great King above all gods." - Psalm 95:1-3

Date_____   Pray For_____

Today's Prayer ✝

_____
_____
_____
_____
_____
_____
_____

Gratitude and Thanks to God for ✝

_____
_____
_____
_____
_____

Take Action (call, write, message) ✝

_____

"Who can find a virtuous woman? for her price is far above rubies." - Proverbs 31:10

Scripture

"O sing unto the LORD a new song: sing unto the LORD, all the earth. Sing unto the LORD, bless his name; shew forth his salvation from day to day. Declare his glory among the heathen, his wonders among all people. For the LORD is great, and greatly to be praised: he is to be feared above all gods." - Psalm 96:1-4

Date _____   Pray For _____

Today's Prayer ✝

_____
_____
_____
_____
_____
_____
_____

Gratitude and Thanks to God for ✝

_____
_____
_____
_____
_____

Take Action (call, write, message) ✝

_____

"Who can find a virtuous woman? for her price is far above rubies." - Proverbs 31:10

"Give unto the LORD, O ye kindreds of the people, give unto the LORD glory and strength. ... O worship the LORD in the beauty of holiness: fear before him, all the earth. ... Let the heavens rejoice, and let the earth be glad; let the sea roar, and the fulness thereof." - Psalm 96:7, 9, 11

Date_____   Pray For_____

Today's Prayer ✝

_____
_____
_____
_____
_____
_____
_____
_____

Gratitude and Thanks to God for ✝

_____
_____
_____
_____
_____

Take Action (call, write, message) ✝

_____

"Who can find a virtuous woman? for her price is far above rubies." - Proverbs 31:10

Scripture

"The LORD reigneth; let the earth rejoice; let the multitude of isles be glad thereof. ... The heavens declare his righteousness, and all the people see his glory. ... Rejoice in the LORD, ye righteous; and give thanks at the remembrance of his holiness." - Psalm 97:1, 6, 12

Date_____ Pray For_____

Today's Prayer ✞

_____
_____
_____
_____
_____
_____
_____

Gratitude and Thanks to God for ✞

_____
_____
_____
_____
_____

Take Action (call, write, message) ✞

_____

"Who can find a virtuous woman? for her price is far above rubies." - Proverbs 31:10

Scripture

"O sing unto the LORD a new song; for he hath done marvellous things: his right hand, and his holy arm, hath gotten him the victory. The LORD hath made known his salvation: his righteousness hath he openly shewed in the sight of the heathen. ... Make a joyful noise unto the LORD, all the earth: make a loud noise, and rejoice, and sing praise." - Psalm 98:1-2, 4

Date_____   Pray For_____

Today's Prayer ✝

_____
_____
_____
_____
_____
_____
_____

Gratitude and Thanks to God for ✝

_____
_____
_____
_____
_____

Take Action (call, write, message) ✝

_____

"Who can find a virtuous woman? for her price is far above rubies." - Proverbs 31:10

Scripture

"Make a joyful noise unto the LORD, all ye lands. Serve the LORD with gladness: come before his presence with singing. ... Enter into his gates with thanksgiving, and into his courts with praise: be thankful unto him, and bless his name. For the LORD is good; his mercy is everlasting; and his truth endureth to all generations." - Psalm 100:1-2, 4-5

Date_____   Pray For_____

Today's Prayer ✝

_____
_____
_____
_____
_____
_____
_____

Gratitude and Thanks to God for ✝

_____
_____
_____
_____
_____

Take Action (call, write, message) ✝

_____

"Who can find a virtuous woman? for her price is far above rubies." - Proverbs 31:10

Scripture

"I will sing of mercy and judgment: unto thee, O LORD, will I sing. I will behave myself wisely in a perfect way. O when wilt thou come unto me? I will walk within my house with a perfect heart. I will set no wicked thing before mine eyes: I hate the work of them that turn aside; it shall not cleave to me." - Psalm 101:1-3

Date_____   Pray For_____

Today's Prayer ♰

_____
_____
_____
_____
_____
_____
_____

Gratitude and Thanks to God for ♰

_____
_____
_____
_____
_____

Take Action (call, write, message) ♰

_____

"Who can find a virtuous woman? for her price is far above rubies." - Proverbs 31:10

Scripture

"Hear my prayer, O LORD, and let my cry come unto thee. Hide not thy face from me in the day when I am in trouble; incline thine ear unto me: in the day when I call answer me speedily. ... But thou, O LORD, shalt endure for ever; and thy remembrance unto all generations." - Psalm 102:1-2, 12

Date_____   Pray For_____

Today's Prayer ✝

_____
_____
_____
_____
_____
_____
_____

Gratitude and Thanks to God for ✝

_____
_____
_____
_____
_____

Take Action (call, write, message) ✝

_____

"Who can find a virtuous woman? for her price is far above rubies." - Proverbs 31:10

Scripture

"[[A Psalm of David.]] Bless the LORD, O my soul: and all that is within me, bless his holy name. Bless the LORD, O my soul, and forget not all his benefits: Who forgiveth all thine iniquities; who healeth all thy diseases; ... The LORD is merciful and gracious, slow to anger, and plenteous in mercy." - Psalm 103:1-3, 8

Date_____   Pray For_____

Today's Prayer ✝

_____
_____
_____
_____
_____
_____
_____

Gratitude and Thanks to God for ✝

_____
_____
_____
_____
_____

Take Action (call, write, message) ✝

_____

"who can find a virtuous woman? for her price is far above rubies." - Proverbs 31:10

Scripture

"Bless the LORD, O my soul. O LORD my God, thou art very great; thou art clothed with honour and majesty. Who covers thyself with light as with a garment: who stretches out the heavens like a curtain: ... I will sing unto the LORD as long as I live: I will sing praise to my God while I have my being. My meditation of him shall be sweet: I will be glad in the LORD." - Psalm 104:1-2, 33-34

Date _____   Pray For _____

Today's Prayer ✝

_____
_____
_____
_____
_____
_____
_____

Gratitude and Thanks to God for ✝

_____
_____
_____
_____
_____

Take Action (call, write, message) ✝

_____

"Who can find a virtuous woman? for her price is far above rubies." - Proverbs 31:10

Scripture

"O give thanks unto the LORD; call upon his name: make known his deeds among the people. Sing unto him, sing psalms unto him: talk ye of all his wondrous works. Glory ye in his holy name: let the heart of them rejoice that seek the LORD. Seek the LORD, and his strength: seek his face evermore." - Psalm 105:1-4

Date _____   Pray For _____

Today's Prayer ✝
_____
_____
_____
_____
_____
_____
_____

Gratitude and Thanks to God for ✝
_____
_____
_____
_____
_____

Take Action (call, write, message) ✝
_____

"Who can find a virtuous woman? for her price is far above rubies." - Proverbs 31:10

Scripture

"Praise ye the LORD. O give thanks unto the LORD; for he is good: for his mercy endureth for ever.... Blessed are they that keep judgment, and he that doeth righteousness at all times. Remember me, O LORD, with the favour that thou bear unto thy people: O visit me with thy salvation;" Psalm 106:1,3-4

Date_____   Pray For_____

Today's Prayer ✝

_____
_____
_____
_____
_____
_____
_____

Gratitude and Thanks to God for ✝

_____
_____
_____
_____
_____

Take Action (call, write, message) ✝

_____

"Who can find a virtuous woman? for her price is far above rubies." - Proverbs 31:10

"O give thanks unto the LORD, for he is good: for his mercy endureth for ever. ... Oh that men would praise the LORD for his goodness, and for his wonderful works to the children of men! ... And let them sacrifice the sacrifices of thanksgiving, and declare his works with rejoicing." - Psalm 107:1, 15, 22

Date_____   Pray For_____

Today's Prayer ✝

_____
_____
_____
_____
_____
_____
_____

Gratitude and Thanks to God for ✝

_____
_____
_____
_____
_____

Take Action (call, write, message) ✝

_____

"Who can find a virtuous woman? for her price is far above rubies." - Proverbs 31:10

Scripture

"I will praise thee, O LORD, among the people: and I will sing praises unto thee among the nations. For thy mercy is great above the heavens: and thy truth reacheth unto the clouds. Be thou exalted, O God, above the heavens: and thy glory above all the earth;" - Psalm 108:3-5

Date_____   Pray For_____

Today's Prayer ✝

_____
_____
_____
_____
_____
_____
_____

Gratitude and Thanks to God for ✝

_____
_____
_____
_____
_____

Take Action (call, write, message) ✝

_____

"Who can find a virtuous woman? for her price is far above rubies." - Proverbs 31:10

Scripture

"Praise ye the LORD. I will praise the LORD with my whole heart, in the assembly of the upright, and in the congregation. The works of the LORD are great, sought out of all them that have pleasure therein. His work is honourable and glorious: and his righteousness endureth for ever." - Psalm 111:1-3

Date_____   Pray For_____

Today's Prayer ✝

_____
_____
_____
_____
_____
_____
_____

Gratitude and Thanks to God for ✝

_____
_____
_____
_____

Take Action (call, write, message) ✝

_____

"Who can find a virtuous woman? for her price is far above rubies." - Proverbs 31:10

Scripture

"He hath made his wonderful works to be remembered: the LORD is gracious and full of compassion... The works of his hands are verity and judgment; all his commandments are sure... The fear of the LORD is the beginning of wisdom: a good understanding have all they that do his commandments: his praise endureth for ever." - Psalm 111:4, 7, 10

Date_____   Pray For_____

Today's Prayer ✞

_____
_____
_____
_____
_____
_____
_____
_____

Gratitude and Thanks to God for ✞

_____
_____
_____
_____
_____

Take Action (call, write, message) ✞

_____

"Who can find a virtuous woman? for her price is far above rubies." - Proverbs 31:10

Scripture

"Praise ye the LORD. Blessed is the man that feareth the LORD, that delighteth greatly in his commandments. His seed shall be mighty upon earth: the generation of the upright shall be blessed. Wealth and riches shall be in his house: and his righteousness endureth for ever." - Psalm 112:1-3

Date _____   Pray For _____

Today's Prayer ✝

_____
_____
_____
_____
_____
_____
_____

Gratitude and Thanks to God for ✝

_____
_____
_____
_____
_____

Take Action (call, write, message) ✝

_____

"Who can find a virtuous woman? for her price is far above rubies." - Proverbs 31:10

Scripture

"Praise ye the LORD. Praise, O ye servants of the LORD, praise the name of the LORD. Blessed be the name of the LORD from this time forth and for evermore. From the rising of the sun unto the going down of the same the LORD'S name is to be praised." - Psalm 113:1-3

Date_____   Pray For_____

Today's Prayer ✝

_____
_____
_____
_____
_____
_____
_____

Gratitude and Thanks to God for ✝

_____
_____
_____
_____
_____

Take Action (call, write, message) ✝

_____

"Who can find a virtuous woman? for her price is far above rubies." - Proverbs 31:10

Scripture

"I love the LORD, because he hath heard my voice and my supplications. Because he hath inclined his ear unto me, therefore will I call upon him as long as I live. ... Gracious is the LORD, and righteous; yea, our God is merciful." - Psalm 116:1-2, 5

Date _____   Pray For _____

Today's Prayer ✝

_____
_____
_____
_____
_____
_____
_____

Gratitude and Thanks to God for ✝

_____
_____
_____
_____
_____

Take Action (call, write, message) ✝

_____

"Who can find a virtuous woman? for her price is far above rubies." - Proverbs 31:10

Scripture

"O give thanks unto the LORD; for he is good: because his mercy endureth for ever. ... Let them now that fear the LORD say, that his mercy endureth for ever. ... The LORD is my strength and song, and is become my salvation." - Psalm 118:1, 4, 14

Date _____   Pray For _____

Today's Prayer ♰

_____
_____
_____
_____
_____
_____
_____

Gratitude and Thanks to God for ♰

_____
_____
_____
_____
_____

Take Action (call, write, message) ♰

_____

"Who can find a virtuous woman? for her price is far above rubies." - Proverbs 31:10

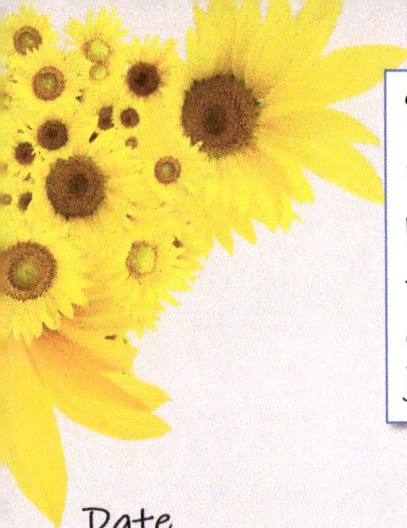

Scripture

"Blessed are they that keep his testimonies, and that seek him with the whole heart. ... O that my ways were directed to keep thy statutes! ... I will praise thee with uprightness of heart, when I shall have learned thy righteous judgments." - Psalm 119:2, 5, 7

Date_____   Pray For_____

Today's Prayer ✝

_____
_____
_____
_____
_____
_____
_____

Gratitude and Thanks to God for ✝

_____
_____
_____
_____
_____

Take Action (call, write, message) ✝

_____

"Who can find a virtuous woman? for her price is far above rubies." - Proverbs 31:10

Scripture

"I will meditate in thy precepts, and have respect unto thy ways. I will delight myself in thy statutes: I will not forget thy word. ... Thy testimonies also are my delight and my counsellors. ... I have chosen the way of truth: thy judgments have I laid before me." - Psalm 119:15-16, 24, 30

Date _____   Pray For _____

Today's Prayer ✝

_____
_____
_____
_____
_____
_____
_____

Gratitude and Thanks to God for ✝

_____
_____
_____
_____
_____

Take Action (call, write, message) ✝

_____

"Who can find a virtuous woman? for her price is far above rubies." - Proverbs 31:10

"I will lift up mine eyes unto the hills, from whence cometh my help. My help cometh from the LORD, which made heaven and earth. ... Behold, he that keepeth Israel shall neither slumber nor sleep. The LORD is thy keeper: the LORD is thy shade upon thy right hand." - Psalm 121:1-2, 4-5

Date_____   Pray For_____

Today's Prayer ✝
_____
_____
_____
_____
_____
_____
_____
_____

Gratitude and Thanks to God for ✝
_____
_____
_____
_____
_____

Take Action (call, write, message) ✝
_____

"Who can find a virtuous woman? for her price is far above rubies." - Proverbs 31:10

Scripture

"I was glad when they said unto me, Let us go into the house of the LORD. Our feet shall stand within thy gates, O Jerusalem. Jerusalem is builded as a city that is compact together: ... Pray for the peace of Jerusalem: they shall prosper that love thee." - Psalm 122:1-3, 6

Date_____   Pray For_____

Today's Prayer ✝

_____
_____
_____
_____
_____
_____
_____

Gratitude and Thanks to God for ✝

_____
_____
_____
_____
_____

Take Action (call, write, message) ✝

_____

"Who can find a virtuous woman? for her price is far above rubies." - Proverbs 31:10

Date_____   Pray For_____

Today's Prayer ✝

_____
_____
_____
_____
_____
_____
_____

Gratitude and Thanks to God for ✝

_____
_____
_____
_____

Take Action (call, write, message) ✝

_____

Scripture

"When the LORD turned again the captivity of Zion, we were like them that dream. Then was our mouth filled with laughter, and our tongue with singing: then said they among the heathen, The LORD hath done great things for them. The LORD hath done great things for us; whereof we are glad." - Psalm 126:1-3 KJV

Date_____ Pray For_____

Today's Prayer ✝

_____
_____
_____
_____
_____
_____
_____
_____

Gratitude and Thanks to God for ✝

_____
_____
_____
_____
_____

Take Action (call, write, message) ✝

_____

"Who can find a virtuous woman? for her price is far above rubies." - Proverbs 31:10

Scripture

"Except the LORD build the house, they labour in vain that build it: except the LORD keep the city, the watchman waketh but in vain. ... Lo, children are an heritage of the LORD: and the fruit of the womb is his reward. As arrows are in the hand of a mighty man; so are children of the youth." - Psalm 127:1, 3-4

Date_____   Pray For_____

Today's Prayer ✝

_____
_____
_____
_____
_____
_____
_____

Gratitude and Thanks to God for ✝

_____
_____
_____
_____

Take Action (call, write, message) ✝

_____

"Who can find a virtuous woman? for her price is far above rubies." - Proverbs 31:10

Scripture

"[A Song of degrees.] Blessed is every one that feareth the LORD; that walketh in his ways. For thou shalt eat the labour of thine hands: happy shalt thou be, and it shall be well with thee... Behold, that thus shall the man be blessed that feareth the LORD. The LORD shall bless thee out of Zion: and thou shalt see the good of Jerusalem all the days of thy life." - Psalm 128:1-2, 4-5

Date_____   Pray For_____

Today's Prayer ✝

_____
_____
_____
_____
_____
_____
_____

Gratitude and Thanks to God for ✝

_____
_____
_____
_____
_____

Take Action (call, write, message) ✝

_____

"Who can find a virtuous woman? for her price is far above rubies." - Proverbs 31:10

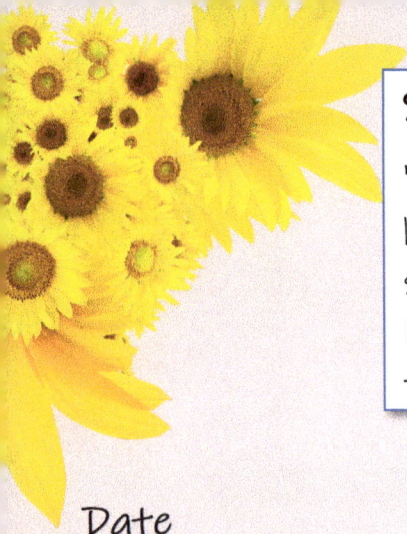

Scripture

"Out of the depths have I cried unto thee, O LORD. Lord, hear my voice: let thine ears be attentive to the voice of my supplications. If thou, LORD, shouldest mark iniquities, O Lord, who shall stand? But there is forgiveness with thee, that thou mayest be feared." - Psalm 130:1-4 KJV

Date_____   Pray For_____

Today's Prayer ✝

_____
_____
_____
_____
_____
_____
_____
_____

Gratitude and Thanks to God for ✝

_____
_____
_____
_____
_____

Take Action (call, write, message) ✝

_____

"Who can find a virtuous woman? for her price is far above rubies." - Proverbs 31:10

Scripture

"I wait for the LORD, my soul doth wait, and in his word do I hope. My soul waiteth for the Lord more than they that watch for the morning: I say, more than they that watch for the morning. Let Israel hope in the LORD: for with the LORD there is mercy, and with him is plenteous redemption." - Psalm 130:5-7

Date_____   Pray For_____

Today's Prayer ✝

_____
_____
_____
_____
_____
_____
_____

Gratitude and Thanks to God for ✝

_____
_____
_____
_____
_____

Take Action (call, write, message) ✝

_____

"Who can find a virtuous woman? for her price is far above rubies." - Proverbs 31:10

Scripture

"For the LORD hath chosen Zion; he hath desired it for his habitation. This is my rest for ever: here will I dwell; for I have desired it. I will abundantly bless her provision: I will satisfy her poor with bread. I will also clothe her priests with salvation: and her saints shall shout aloud for joy." - Psalm 132:13-16

Date_____   Pray For_____

Today's Prayer ✝

_____
_____
_____
_____
_____
_____
_____
_____

Gratitude and Thanks to God for ✝

_____
_____
_____
_____

Take Action (call, write, message) ✝

_____

"Who can find a virtuous woman? for her price is far above rubies." - Proverbs 31:10

Scripture

"Behold, how good and how pleasant it is for brethren to dwell together in unity! It is like the precious ointment upon the head, that ran down upon the beard, even Aaron's beard: that went down to the skirts of his garments... for there the LORD commanded the blessing, even life for evermore." - Psalm 133:1-3

Date_____   Pray For_____

Today's Prayer ✟

_____
_____
_____
_____
_____
_____
_____
_____

Gratitude and Thanks to God for ✟

_____
_____
_____
_____

Take Action (call, write, message) ✟

_____

"Who can find a virtuous woman? for her price is far above rubies." - Proverbs 31:10

Scripture

"Behold, bless ye the LORD, all ye servants of the LORD, which by night stand in the house of the LORD. Lift up your hands in the sanctuary, and bless the LORD. The LORD that made heaven and earth bless thee out of Zion." - Psalm 134:1-3

Date_____   Pray For_____

Today's Prayer ✝
_____
_____
_____
_____
_____
_____
_____

Gratitude and Thanks to God for ✝
_____
_____
_____
_____
_____

Take Action (call, write, message) ✝
_____

"Who can find a virtuous woman? for her price is far above rubies." - Proverbs 31:10

Scripture

"Praise ye the LORD. Praise ye the name of the LORD; praise him, O ye servants of the LORD. Ye that stand in the house of the LORD, in the courts of the house of our God, Praise the LORD; for the LORD is good: sing praises unto his name; for it is pleasant." - Psalm 135:1-3

Date_____   Pray For_____

Today's Prayer ✝

_____

_____

_____

_____

_____

_____

Gratitude and Thanks to God for ✝

_____

_____

_____

_____

Take Action (call, write, message) ✝

_____

"Who can find a virtuous woman? for her price is far above rubies." - Proverbs 31:10

Scripture

"For I know that the LORD is great, and that our Lord is above all gods. Whatsoever the LORD pleased, that did he in heaven, and in earth, in the seas, and all deep places. ... Thy name, O LORD, endureth for ever; and thy memorial, O LORD, throughout all generations." - Psalm 135:5-6, 13

Date_____   Pray For_____

Today's Prayer ✝

_____
_____
_____
_____
_____
_____
_____

Gratitude and Thanks to God for ✝

_____
_____
_____
_____
_____

Take Action (call, write, message) ✝

_____

Scripture

"O give thanks unto the LORD; for he is good: for his mercy endureth for ever. ... To him who alone doeth great wonders: for his mercy endureth for ever. To him that by wisdom made the heavens: for his mercy endureth for ever." - Psalm 136:1, 4-5 KJV

Date_____   Pray For_____

Today's Prayer ✝

_____
_____
_____
_____
_____
_____
_____

Gratitude and Thanks to God for ✝

_____
_____
_____
_____
_____

Take Action (call, write, message) ✝

_____

"Who can find a virtuous woman? for her price is far above rubies." - Proverbs 31:10

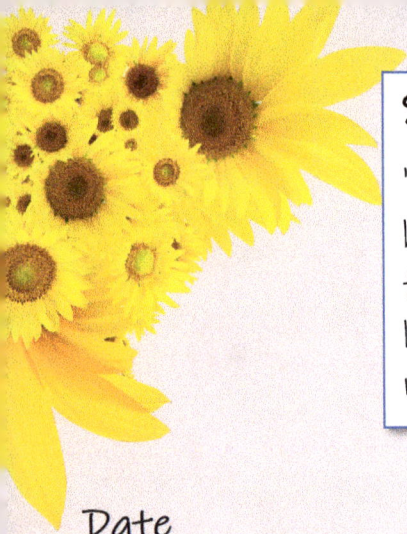

Scripture

"To him that stretched out the earth above the waters: for his mercy endureth for ever. To him that made great lights: for his mercy endureth for ever: The sun to rule by day: for his mercy endureth for ever: The moon and stars to rule by night: for his mercy endureth for ever." - Psalm 136:6-9 KJV

Date_____   Pray For_____

Today's Prayer ✝

_____
_____
_____
_____
_____
_____
_____

Gratitude and Thanks to God for ✝

_____
_____
_____
_____
_____

Take Action (call, write, message) ✝

_____

"Who can find a virtuous woman? for her price is far above rubies." - Proverbs 31:10

Scripture

"I will praise thee with my whole heart: before the gods will I sing praise unto thee. I will worship toward thy holy temple, and praise thy name for thy lovingkindness and for thy truth: for thou hast magnified thy word above all thy name. In the day when I cried thou answeredst me, and strengthenedst me with strength in my soul." - Psalm 138:1-3

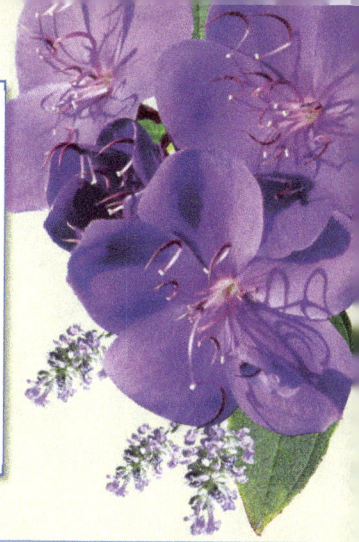

Date_____   Pray For_____

Today's Prayer ✠

_____
_____
_____
_____
_____
_____
_____
_____

Gratitude and Thanks to God for ✠

_____
_____
_____
_____
_____

Take Action (call, write, message) ✠

_____

"Who can find a virtuous woman? for her price is far above rubies." - Proverbs 31:10

Scripture

"All the kings of the earth shall praise thee, O LORD, when they hear the words of thy mouth. Yea, they shall sing in the ways of the LORD: for great is the glory of the LORD. Though the LORD be high, yet hath he respect unto the lowly: but the proud he knoweth afar off." - Psalm 138:4-6

Date_____   Pray For_____

Today's Prayer ✝

_____
_____
_____
_____
_____
_____
_____

Gratitude and Thanks to God for ✝

_____
_____
_____
_____

Take Action (call, write, message) ✝

_____

"Who can find a virtuous woman? for her price is far above rubies." - Proverbs 31:10

Scripture

"O LORD, thou hast searched me, and known me. Thou knowest my downsitting and mine uprising, thou understandest my thought afar off. Thou compassest my path and my lying down, and art acquainted with all my ways. For there is not a word in my tongue, but, lo, O LORD, thou knowest it altogether." - Psalm 139:1-4

Date_____   Pray For_____

Today's Prayer ✝

_____
_____
_____
_____
_____
_____
_____
_____

Gratitude and Thanks to God for ✝

_____
_____
_____
_____
_____

Take Action (call, write, message) ✝

_____

"Who can find a virtuous woman? for her price is far above rubies." - Proverbs 31:10

Scripture

"If I ascend up into heaven, thou art there: if I make my bed in hell, behold, thou art there. If I take the wings of the morning, and dwell in the uttermost parts of the sea; Even there shall thy hand lead me, and thy right hand shall hold me." - Psalm 139:8-10

Date _____   Pray For _____

Today's Prayer ✝

_____
_____
_____
_____
_____
_____
_____

Gratitude and Thanks to God for ✝

_____
_____
_____
_____
_____

Take Action (call, write, message) ✝

_____

"Who can find a virtuous woman? for her price is far above rubies." - Proverbs 31:10

Scripture

"I will praise thee; for I am fearfully and wonderfully made: marvellous are thy works; and that my soul knoweth right well. My substance was not hid from thee, when I was made in secret, and curiously wrought in the lowest parts of the earth. ... How precious also are thy thoughts unto me, O God! how great is the sum of them!" - Psalm 139:14-15, 17

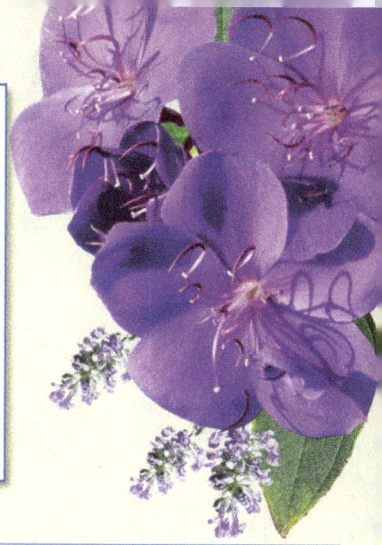

Date_____   Pray For_____

Today's Prayer ✝

_____
_____
_____
_____
_____
_____
_____
_____

Gratitude and Thanks to God for ✝

_____
_____
_____
_____
_____

Take Action (call, write, message) ✝

_____

"Who can find a virtuous woman? for her price is far above rubies." - Proverbs 31:10

Scripture .

"If I ascend up into heaven, thou art there: if I make my bed in hell, behold, thou art there. ... Search me, O God, and know my heart: try me, and know my thoughts: And see if there be any wicked way in me, and lead me in the way everlasting." - Psalm 139:8, 23-24 KJV

Date_____   Pray For_____

Today's Prayer ☦

_____
_____
_____
_____
_____
_____
_____

Gratitude and Thanks to God for ☦

_____
_____
_____
_____
_____

Take Action (call, write, message) ☦

_____

"Who can find a virtuous woman? for her price is far above rubies." - Proverbs 31:10

Scripture

"I said unto the LORD, Thou art my God: hear the voice of my supplications, O LORD. O GOD the Lord, the strength of my salvation, thou hast covered my head in the day of battle. ... Surely the righteous shall give thanks unto thy name: the upright shall dwell in thy presence." - Psalm 140:6-7, 13

Date_____ Pray For_____

Today's Prayer ✝

_____
_____
_____
_____
_____
_____
_____

Gratitude and Thanks to God for ✝

_____
_____
_____
_____
_____

Take Action (call, write, message) ✝

_____

"Who can find a virtuous woman? for her price is far above rubies." - Proverbs 31:10

Scripture

"[A Psalm of David.] LORD, I cry unto thee: make haste unto me; give ear unto my voice, when I cry unto thee. Let my prayer be set forth before thee as incense; and the lifting up of my hands as the evening sacrifice. Set a watch, O LORD, before my mouth; keep the door of my lips." - Psalm 141:1-3

Date_____   Pray For_____

Today's Prayer ✝

_____
_____
_____
_____
_____
_____
_____

Gratitude and Thanks to God for ✝

_____
_____
_____
_____
_____

Take Action (call, write, message) ✝

_____

"Who can find a virtuous woman? for her price is far above rubies." - Proverbs 31:10

Scripture

"A Prayer when he was in the cave.] I cried unto the LORD with my voice; with my voice unto the LORD did I make my supplication. I poured out my complaint before him; I shewed before him my trouble. ... I cried unto thee, O LORD: I said, Thou art my refuge and my portion in the land of the living. ... for thou shalt deal bountifully with me." - Psalm 142:1-2, 5, 7

Date_____   Pray For_____

Today's Prayer ✝

_____
_____
_____
_____
_____
_____
_____

Gratitude and Thanks to God for ✝

_____
_____
_____
_____
_____

Take Action (call, write, message) ✝

_____

"Who can find a virtuous woman? for her price is far above rubies." - Proverbs 31:10

Scripture

"Hear my prayer, O LORD, give ear to my supplications: in thy faithfulness answer me, and in thy righteousness. And enter not into judgment with thy servant: for in thy sight shall no man living be justified. ... Teach me to do thy will; for thou art my God: thy spirit is good; lead me into the land of uprightness."
- Psalm 143:1-2, 10

Date_____ Pray For_____

Today's Prayer ✝

_____
_____
_____
_____
_____
_____
_____

Gratitude and Thanks to God for ✝

_____
_____
_____
_____
_____

Take Action (call, write, message) ✝

_____

"Who can find a virtuous woman? for her price is far above rubies." - Proverbs 31:10

Scripture

"LORD, what is man, that thou takest knowledge of him! or the son of man, that thou makest account of him! ... I will sing a new song unto thee, O God: upon a psaltery and an instrument of ten strings will I sing praises unto thee. ... Happy is that people, that is in such a case: yea, happy is that people, whose God is the LORD." - Psalm 144:3, 9, 15

Date_____   Pray For_____

Today's Prayer ✝

_____
_____
_____
_____
_____
_____
_____

Gratitude and Thanks to God for ✝

_____
_____
_____
_____
_____

Take Action (call, write, message) ✝

_____

"Who can find a virtuous woman? for her price is far above rubies." - Proverbs 31:10

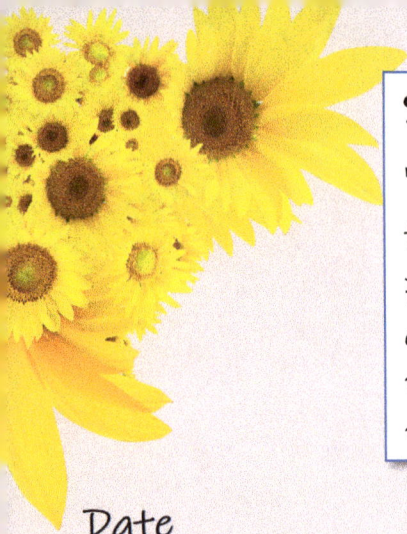

Scripture

"I will extol thee, my God, O king; and I will bless thy name for ever and ever. Every day will I bless thee; and I will praise thy name for ever and ever. Great is the LORD, and greatly to be praised; and his greatness is unsearchable. ... I will speak of the glorious honour of thy majesty, and of thy wondrous works." - Psalm 145:1-3, 5

Date_____   Pray For_____

Today's Prayer ✝

_____
_____
_____
_____
_____
_____
_____

Gratitude and Thanks to God for ✝

_____
_____
_____
_____
_____

Take Action (call, write, message) ✝

_____

"Who can find a virtuous woman? for her price is far above rubies." - Proverbs 31:10

Scripture

"The LORD is gracious, and full of compassion; slow to anger, and of great mercy. The LORD is good to all: and his tender mercies are over all his works. All thy works shall praise thee, O LORD; and thy saints shall bless thee." - Psalm 145:8-10

Date_____ Pray For_____

Today's Prayer ✝

_____
_____
_____
_____
_____
_____
_____

Gratitude and Thanks to God for ✝

_____
_____
_____
_____

Take Action (call, write, message) ✝

_____

"Who can find a virtuous woman? for her price is far above rubies." - Proverbs 31:10

Scripture

"They shall speak of the glory of thy kingdom, and talk of thy power; To make known to the sons of men his mighty acts, and the glorious majesty of his kingdom. Thy kingdom is an everlasting kingdom, and thy dominion endureth throughout all generations." - Psalm 145:11-13

Date_____   Pray For_____

Today's Prayer ✝

_____
_____
_____
_____
_____
_____
_____

Gratitude and Thanks to God for ✝

_____
_____
_____
_____
_____

Take Action (call, write, message) ✝

_____

"Who can find a virtuous woman? for her price is far above rubies." - Proverbs 31:10

Scripture

"The LORD upholdeth all that fall, and raiseth up all those that be bowed down. ... Thou openest thine hand, and satisfiest the desire of every living thing. The LORD is righteous in all his ways, and holy in all his works." - Psalm 145:14, 16–17

Date _____ Pray For _____

Today's Prayer ✝

_____
_____
_____
_____
_____
_____
_____
_____

Gratitude and Thanks to God for ✝

_____
_____
_____
_____
_____

Take Action (call, write, message) ✝

_____

"Who can find a virtuous woman? for her price is far above rubies." - Proverbs 31:10

Scripture

"The LORD is nigh unto all them that call upon him, to all that call upon him in truth. He will fulfil the desire of them that fear him: he also will hear their cry, and will save them. The LORD preserveth all them that love him: but all the wicked will he destroy." - Psalm 145:18-20

Date_____   Pray For_____

Today's Prayer ✞

_____
_____
_____
_____
_____
_____
_____

Gratitude and Thanks to God for ✞

_____
_____
_____
_____
_____

Take Action (call, write, message) ✞

_____

"Who can find a virtuous woman? for her price is far above rubies." - Proverbs 31:10

Scripture

"Praise ye the LORD. Praise the LORD, O my soul. While I live will I praise the LORD: I will sing praises unto my God while I have any being. ... Happy is he that hath the God of Jacob for his help, whose hope is in the LORD his God:" - Psalm 146:1-2, 5

Date_____   Pray For_____

Today's Prayer ✞

_____
_____
_____
_____
_____
_____
_____

Gratitude and Thanks to God for ✞

_____
_____
_____
_____
_____

Take Action (call, write, message) ✞

_____

"Who can find a virtuous woman? for her price is far above rubies." - Proverbs 31:10

Scripture

"The LORD openeth the eyes of the blind: the LORD raiseth them that are bowed down: the LORD loveth the righteous: The LORD preserveth the strangers; he relieveth the fatherless and widow... The LORD shall reign for ever, even thy God, O Zion, unto all generations. Praise ye the LORD." - Psalm 146:8-10

Date_____   Pray For_____

Today's Prayer ✝

_____
_____
_____
_____
_____
_____
_____

Gratitude and Thanks to God for ✝

_____
_____
_____
_____
_____

Take Action (call, write, message) ✝

_____

"Who can find a virtuous woman? for her price is far above rubies." - Proverbs 31:10

Scripture

"Praise ye the LORD: for it is good to sing praises unto our God; for it is pleasant; and praise is comely. ... He healeth the broken in heart, and bindeth up their wounds. ... Great is our Lord, and of great power: his understanding is infinite." - Psalm 147:1, 3, 5 KJV

Date_____ Pray For_____

Today's Prayer ✝

_____
_____
_____
_____
_____
_____
_____

Gratitude and Thanks to God for ✝

_____
_____
_____
_____
_____

Take Action (call, write, message) ✝

_____

"Who can find a virtuous woman? for her price is far above rubies." - Proverbs 31:10

Date_____   Pray For_____

Today's Prayer ✝

_____
_____
_____
_____
_____
_____
_____

Gratitude and Thanks to God for ✝

_____
_____
_____
_____

Take Action (call, write, message) ✝

_____

Scripture

"Praise ye the LORD. Praise ye the LORD from the heavens: praise him in the heights. Praise ye him, all his angels: praise ye him, all his hosts. Praise ye him, sun and moon: praise him, all ye stars of light. Praise him, ye heavens of heavens, and ye waters that be above the heavens." - Psalm 148:1-4

Date_____   Pray For_____

Today's Prayer ✝

_____
_____
_____
_____
_____
_____
_____

Gratitude and Thanks to God for ✝

_____
_____
_____
_____
_____

Take Action (call, write, message) ✝

_____

"Who can find a virtuous woman? for her price is far above rubies." - Proverbs 31:10

Scripture

"Let them praise the name of the LORD: for he commanded, and they were created. He hath also stablished them for ever and ever: he hath made a decree which shall not pass. ... Let them praise the name of the LORD: for his name alone is excellent; his glory is above the earth and heaven." - Psalm 148:5-6, 13

Date_____ Pray For_____

Today's Prayer ☨

_____
_____
_____
_____
_____
_____
_____
_____

Gratitude and Thanks to God for ☨

_____
_____
_____
_____
_____

Take Action (call, write, message) ☨

_____

"Who can find a virtuous woman? for her price is far above rubies." - Proverbs 31:10

Scripture

"Praise ye the LORD. Sing unto the LORD a new song, and his praise in the congregation of saints. ... Let them praise his name in the dance: let them sing praises unto him with the timbrel and harp. For the LORD taketh pleasure in his people: he will beautify the meek with salvation." - Psalm 149:1, 3-4

Date _____   Pray For _____

Today's Prayer ✞

_____
_____
_____
_____
_____
_____
_____

Gratitude and Thanks to God for ✞

_____
_____
_____
_____

Take Action (call, write, message) ✞

_____

"Who can find a virtuous woman? for her price is far above rubies." - Proverbs 31:10

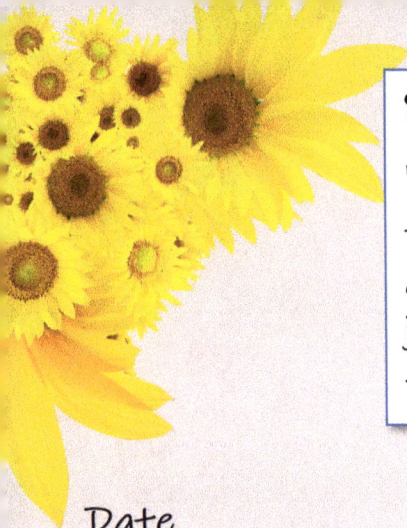

Scripture

"Let the saints be joyful in glory: let them sing aloud upon their beds. Let the high praises of God be in their mouth, and a twoedged sword in their hand; ... To execute upon them the judgment written: this honour have all his saints. Praise ye the LORD." - Psalm 149:5-6, 9

Date _____   Pray For _____

Today's Prayer ✝

_____
_____
_____
_____
_____
_____
_____

Gratitude and Thanks to God for ✝

_____
_____
_____
_____
_____

Take Action (call, write, message) ✝

_____

"who can find a virtuous woman? for her price is far above rubies." - Proverbs 31:10

Scripture

"Praise ye the LORD. Praise God in his sanctuary: praise him in the firmament of his power. Praise him for his mighty acts: praise him according to his excellent greatness. Praise him with the sound of the trumpet: praise him with the psaltery and harp." - Psalm 150:1-3

Date_____   Pray For_____

Today's Prayer ♰

_____
_____
_____
_____
_____
_____
_____

Gratitude and Thanks to God for ♰

_____
_____
_____
_____
_____

Take Action (call, write, message) ♰

_____

"Who can find a virtuous woman? for her price is far above rubies." - Proverbs 31:10

Scripture

"Praise him with the timbrel and dance: praise him with stringed instruments and organs. Praise him upon the loud cymbals: praise him upon the high sounding cymbals. Let every thing that hath breath praise the LORD. Praise ye the LORD." - Psalm 150:4-6

Date_____   Pray For_____

Today's Prayer ✝

_____
_____
_____
_____
_____
_____
_____
_____

Gratitude and Thanks to God for ✝

_____
_____
_____
_____
_____

Take Action (call, write, message) ✝

_____

"Who can find a virtuous woman? for her price is far above rubies." - Proverbs 31:10

www.ingramcontent.com/pod-product-compliance
Lightning Source LLC
Chambersburg PA
CBHW050617110426
42813CB00008B/2589